D1372172

LIFE EDUCATION

An Amazing Machine

Written by
Alexandra Parsons

Illustrated by
John Shackell, Stuart Harrison
and Paul Banville

FRANKLIN WATTS
A DIVISION OF GROLIER PUBLISHING
NEW YORK • LONDON • HONG KONG • SYDNEY
DANBURY, CONNECTICUT

First American Edition
© 1996 by Franklin Watts
A Division of Grolier Publishing
Sherman Turnpike
Danbury, Connecticut
06816

10 9 8 7 6 5 4 3 2 1

Library of Congress Cataloging-in-Publication Data
Parsons, Alex
    An amazing machine / by Alexandra Parsons.
      p. cm. — (Life education)
    Includes index.
    Summary: Provides an overview of various body
systems, including the skeleton, nervous system,
skin, digestion, and more, and how they function.
      ISBN 0-531-14375-9 (lib. bdg.)
      1. Human anatomy —Juvenile literature [1.
Body, Human. 2. Human physiology.] I. Title.
II. Series.
    OM27. P274 1995
    612—dc20   95-20911
                                                  CIP AC

Edited by: Janet De Saulles
Designed by: Sally Boothroyd
Commissioned photography by: Steve Shott
Illustrations by: John Shackell, Paul Banville,
and Stuart Harrison
Consultant for anatomical illustrations:
Dr. Sue Crimlisk

Acknowledgments:
Commissioned photography by Steve Shott: title
page; contents page; 4 (all); 5 (all); 6; 10 (both); 11
(both); 12; 13; 15; 18; 19; 22. Researched
photographs: Science Photo Library 9 (bottom); 17;
21.
Artwork: all cartoon illustrations of "alien" by Stuart
Harrison. Other cartoon illustrations by John
Shackell: cover; 8/9 (center); 14 (right & bottom);
16 (bottom); 20 (bottom); 23 (left); 24 (both); 25
(all); 26 (top); 27 (top); 28 (both); 29 (both).
Anatomical illustrations by Paul Banville: 6 (all); 7
(all); 8 (left); 9 (right); 10 (all); 11 (all); 12 (both);
13; 14 (center-top); 15 (all); 16 (top); 18 (top); 20
(top); 22 (top).

Watts Books and Life Education International are
indebted to Vince Hatton and Laurie Noffs for their
invaluable help.

The publisher would like to extend special thanks to
all the actors who appear in the *Life Education* books
(Key Stage 2):
Jessamy Heath   Danny Mancini
Dishni Payagale Don   Peter Wood
Young-min Kim   Stephen Miles
Debbie Okangi   Daisy Doodles
Michael Wood   Joseph Wood
Mark Wall   Simon Wall
Andrew Wall   Christopher Wall
Vanessa Neita   Amber Neita-Crowley
Jun King   Ken King
Ben Clewley

"*Each second we live is a new and unique moment of the
universe, a moment that will never be again....And what do
we teach our children? We teach them that two and two make
four and that Paris is the capital of France.*

*When will we also teach them: do you know who you are? You
are a marvel. You are unique. In all the years that have
passed, there has never been another child like you. And look
at your body – what a wonder it is! Your legs, your arms, your
clever fingers, the way you move. You may become a
Shakespeare, a Michelangelo, a Beethoven. You have the
capacity for anything. Yes, you are a marvel. And when you
grow up, can you then harm another who is, like you, a
marvel? You must cherish one another. You must work – we
must all work – to make this world worthy of its children.*"

Pablo Casals

Hi! I'm Zapp.
Excuse the intrusion.
Just popped over from
Pluto to check you
all out.

CONTENTS

Your body is an incredible piece of living machinery. You have 206 bones as strong as granite; more than 650 muscles to help you bend and stretch; 10,000 taste buds so you can enjoy your food; 60,000 miles (100,000 km) of blood vessels to keep vital supplies rushing to every part of your body, and millions of brain cells sending out messages at a rate of over 250 mph (400 kph). On top of all this amazing activity, your body is busy growing and changing.

FROM BABY . . .

When you were a baby, you spent your time filling your tummy with milk, crying, and sleeping. But while you were doing that, your body and your brain were busy growing and learning.

At about 6 months old, babies learn to crawl. They start to take an interest in their surroundings. First teeth have already started to appear, and parents can start feeding them solid foods.

Age 1, body weight has tripled. Muscles are strong enough to start learning to walk.

At about 18 months, toddlers can walk and even run (although they often trip!) and are starting to learn to speak.

Age 3, arms and legs are longer and stronger. Children are beginning to coordinate their movements, and should be able to throw a ball, hold a crayon and maybe write their names. At 4 years old, children have a full set of twenty first teeth. Permanent teeth are growing in the gums. Four-year-olds are very aware of the world around them, and are always asking why? Why?

You're Growing!

✓ Each fingernail takes about 6 months to grow from base to tip.

✓ Every night you get longer as you sleep, shrinking back to where you should be when you get up in the morning. This is because the pads between the bones in your spine get squashed when you stand up, but have a chance to expand a bit as you lie down.

Between 7 and 10, growth rate slows down and then speeds up again as puberty approaches. First teeth start to fall out and permanent teeth appear.

Between the ages of about 9 and 15, children's bodies change to adult bodies. These changes, which make it possible for females and males to make babies of their own, occur during a time called puberty. After puberty, bones stop growing but muscles are still building.

. . . TO ADULT

Will you be tall or short? That depends on how tall your parents are and on how much good food you eat. The human race is growing taller as many people's diets improve. We Plutons, on the other hand, all measure precisely the same, which makes shopping for clothes very easy.

. . . . UNDER MY SKIN . . . .

T he remarkable things going on inside your body are organized into different systems. Each system does a particular job, but they are all linked together and one system cannot work without the others.

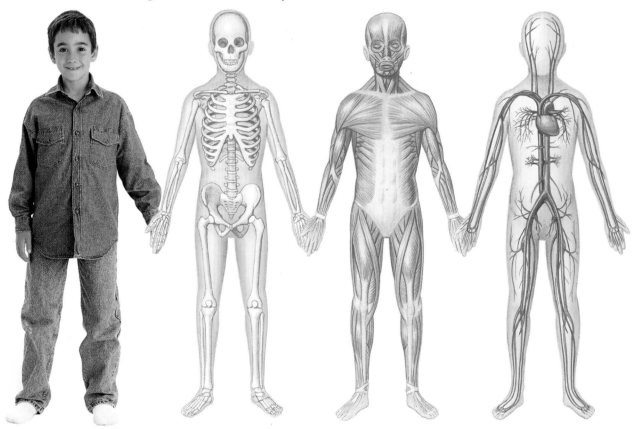

THE SKELETAL SYSTEM,
or skeleton, is the bony framework of the body.

THE MUSCLE SYSTEM
holds bones together and makes it possible for us to move.

THE CIRCULATORY SYSTEM
pushes blood around the body, delivering oxygen and nutrients.

WHAT IS A CELL?
Your body is made up of millions of tiny units called cells. Different kinds of cells join together to make up the different systems:

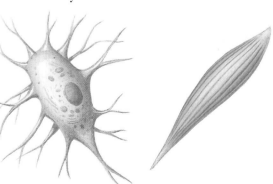

Bones are made up of bone cells.

Muscles are made from bundles of muscle fibers.

Blood is made from blood cells.

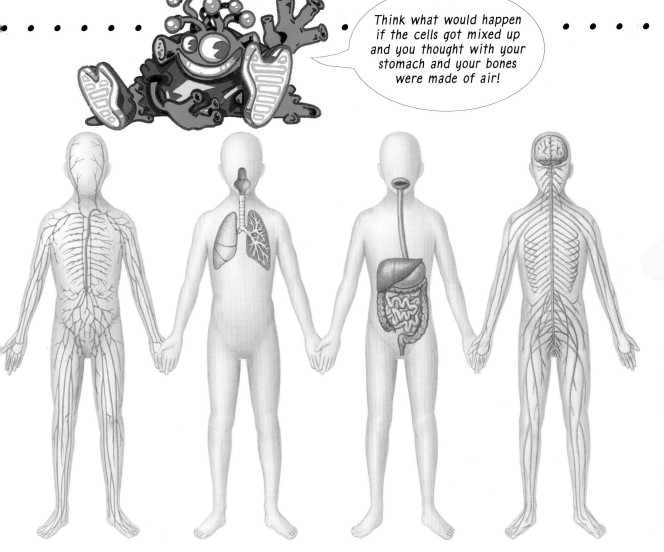

Think what would happen if the cells got mixed up and you thought with your stomach and your bones were made of air!

THE IMMUNE SYSTEM
helps your body fight off disease.

THE RESPIRATORY SYSTEM
brings oxygen into the body.

THE DIGESTIVE SYSTEM
takes nutrients from the food we eat and turns it into fuel the body can use.

THE NERVOUS SYSTEM,
headed up by the brain, is the body's control center.

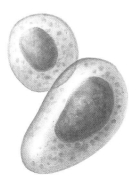

Special blood cells called T-cells help your body fight disease.

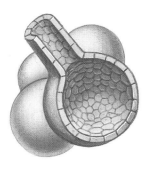

Lungs are made from little sacs of air.

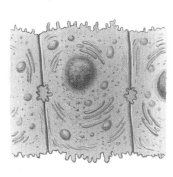

Livers are made from liver cells.

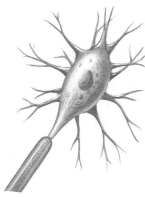

Nerves are made from nerve cells.

Try to imagine what your body would be like with no bones. A flabby blob! But bones are not there just to give you shape and help you move around; their other job is to protect the most important parts, called organs, inside you. Your skull, which is in fact a complicated jigsaw puzzle made up from 22 pieces, protects your precious brain. Your ribcage protects your heart and lungs. Your backbone protects your spinal cord — the major nerve corridor.

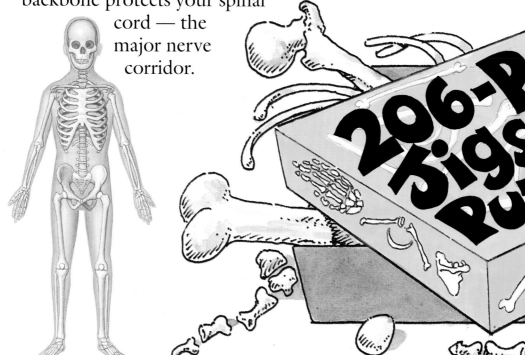

The skeletal system.

DIFFERENT KINDS OF BONE

Each bone looks different because it has a special job to do. You've got long narrow bones in your legs and arms so you can make big movements, and lots of little bones in your feet and hands so you can make delicate movements – like wiggling your toes or picking up a pin.

WHAT'S IN A BONE?

Bones are not solid. They are built like a honeycomb, so they have both strength and lightness. Some bones have hollow spaces inside, filled with a jellylike substance called bone marrow. Marrow is like a little factory making blood cells that the blood picks up as it passes by.

BREAKING BONES

Bones do get broken, but the good news is they can mend! Because bones are made of living cells, new bone will grow and knit the broken ends together. The broken bone needs to be kept very still while this process is going on. People with broken arms and legs are often given plaster casts to make sure the bones mend properly.

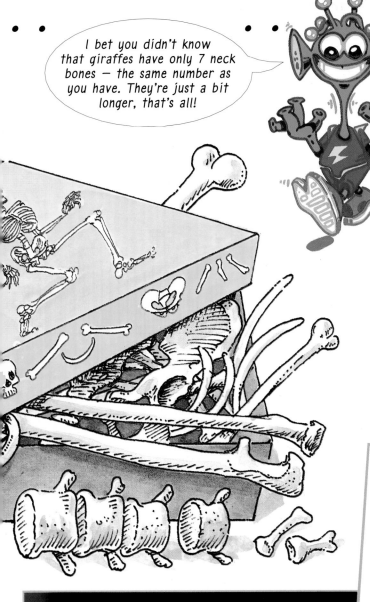

I bet you didn't know that giraffes have only 7 neck bones — the same number as you have. They're just a bit longer, that's all!

The spine and pelvic bones together make a strong but light structure. They can support heavy weights and withstand a great deal of stress. Our skeletons are a magnificent work of engineering.

This is an X-Ray picture of a broken collar bone. The bone will take about three weeks to mend.

Your Super Skeleton

✓ The smallest bone in the body is a little bone inside your ear, called the stirrup bone. It is about the size of a pea.

✓ The largest bone in the body is the femur, or thighbone.

✓ You have 27 bones in each hand.

✓ Children's bones mend more quickly than adults' bones. Hurrah!

✓ Babies are born with about 350 bones. As they grow, some of the bones join together to make bigger bones, and they end up with 206, just like everybody else!

9

You may have noticed that you can't move your elbow sideways or backward, but you can move your whole arm around in a circle. This is because you have different kinds of joints between your bones, each designed to do different things.

WHAT IS A JOINT?

It is where two or more bones meet. Bones have a special coating called cartilage, that covers the ends of bones that move and touch. Cartilage does not get worn away. Your nose has cartilage inside instead of bone. Push your nose from side to side and you can feel how strong yet flexible cartilage actually is.

Bones are attached to other bones by ligaments, which are like little bundles of string. Tendons are strong cords that attach muscle to bone. Bones don't move on their own — it's your muscles that make them move!

LET'S START AT THE TOP!

Twenty-one of the twenty-two bones in your skull are fixed. They do not move.

The hinge joints on either side of your lower jaw bone are the only moving joints in your skull. They move the jaw up and down and sideways just a little. Try it!

SHOULDERS AND HIPS

These are ball-and-socket joints, where a long bone meets a bony structure. The long bone ends in a ball shape that fits into a snug, round hollow. You should be able to move your arms and legs in a circle. Try it!

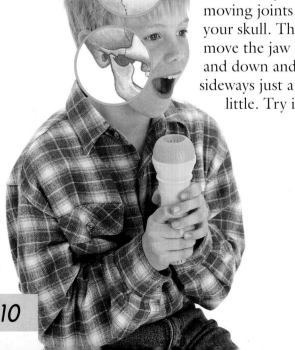

Imagine what would happen if you had the wrong kinds of joints in the wrong places! How would you walk if your knees could bend backward like mine?

Your Jumping Joints

✓ Hip, shoulder, and knee joints can get diseased and crumbly, but they can be replaced with artificial joints made of steel and special plastics.

✓ There are over 100 joints in the adult human body.

✓ Hands and feet have almost the same arrangement of bones, but the joints in the hand are more flexible. Some people who have lost the use of their hands have been able, with a lot of practice, to use their feet to use a keyboard, write, and paint.

ELBOWS AND KNEES

These are hinge joints that move the lower arm and lower leg backward and forward. There is a little movement from side to side, but not much. Try it!

ANKLES AND WRISTS

These joints are made up of lots of little bones so they can move this way and that. You can move your hands and feet in many ways. Try it!

11

Walking, jumping, running, swimming, balancing, throwing, and catching — just think of all the movements your amazing body can make. It is thanks to your muscles that all these movements are possible. There are more than 650 of them, all working hard so that you can run around, sit watching television (there are muscles around your eyes), or smile and laugh with your friends.

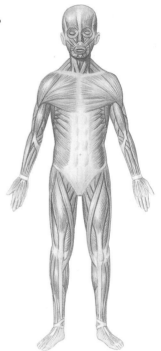

The muscle system.

PUSHING AND PULLING

Muscles that move major joints often work in pairs. This is because muscles cannot push, only pull. So as one muscle pulls, the other relaxes and stretches. To make the joint bend the other way, the muscle that was pulling relaxes, and the muscle that was relaxing pulls!

MUSCLE SHEETS

Not all muscles move bones. Some are there to hold organs in place and give you shape. Your stomach muscles, for instance, consist of three layers of muscle.

MESSAGE TO MOVE

Muscles move because the brain tells them to. The brain sends signals through nerve endings.

You have no bones to strengthen your stomach, you have three layers of sheet muscle instead.

MUSCLE FUEL

Muscles get their energy from the body's blood supply. This delivers them oxygen from the air we breathe and nutrients from the food we eat.

YOU HAVE MUSCLES IN PLACES YOU DIDN'T EVEN KNOW ABOUT!

There are tiny little muscles inside your blood vessels that push your blood around. There are muscles inside your stomach and intestines, squashing and pushing your food through the digestive system. You don't have to think about moving these muscles — the brain takes care of it all automatically!

THE MOST IMPORTANT MUSCLE OF ALL

Your heart is a muscle. It is made from a very special type of muscle called cardiac muscle. It beats regularly without having to be told what to do by the brain.

As muscles pull, they get shorter and fatter, bunching up under the skin.

You humans use 17 muscles to smile and 43 to frown.

Your Marvelous Muscles

✓ The more you use your muscles, the stronger and more powerful they become.

✓ Muscles account for almost half our body weight.

✓ The smallest human muscle is in the ear. It is about $1/25$ of an inch (1 mm) long.

✓ The muscles we use to focus our eyes move about 100,000 times a day.

✓ Some of the body's most flexible muscles are in the tongue. Try saying "Red leather, yellow leather" over and over again really, really fast – feel your tongue working overtime!

✓ Hiccups happen when the diaphragm (the muscle that plays a role in breathing) contracts suddenly, forcing us to breathe in sharply, again and again.

13

W here do you think your breakfast is now? It has become part of you! All the food and drink you consume goes through your digestive system. The job of your digestive system is to turn what you eat and drink into the fuel your body needs to keep all these complicated systems ticking along.

We eat about 1,100 pounds (500 kg) of food per year and about 66,000 pounds (30,000 kg) in a lifetime. That's a pile of food weighing the same as six elephants.

Your Dynamite Digestion

✓ *The stomach is lined with 35 million glands that produce approximately 3 quarts (2.85 liters) of digestive juices every day.*

✓ *Some digestive juices are strong acids — so strong they could burn through metal. Luckily the stomach has a special lining that stops the acids from getting out. This lining renews itself every three days.*

KEY
*red trucks = blood
yellow dots = oxygen
green dots = nutrients*

FIRST STOP ▶
The digestive process starts in the mouth. As you chew your cereal or toast, the liquid in your mouth, called saliva, starts working on the food. You swallow little pieces of softened-up food.

THIRD STOP ▶
The "soup" enters the small intestine, a great long tube that twists and turns for about 20 feet (6 meters). Your breakfast travels through this tube, a journey that can take from 1 to 6 hours. There are tiny feathery fingers, called villi, on the inside wall of your intestine. Villi soak up all the nourishment from your breakfast and pass it into the blood supply. These villi are not very fussy — they take everything you give them. If, for instance, you had a bag of greasy potato chips and a sugary drink for breakfast, your blood would be overdosed with fat and sugar and you wouldn't be feeling very well.

The digestive system.

SMALL INTESTINE
VILLI
BLOOD SUPPLY

Nutrients from food are passed into the blood stream by the villi that line the small intestine.

SECOND STOP

Ten seconds later, the little pieces land in your stomach, where they are churned around with powerful digestive juices. After about 1 to 4 hours, depending on how easy the food is to digest, your breakfast is ready to leave the stomach. By now it has been reduced to a creamy, souplike liquid.

LAST STOP

Food that cannot pass into the blood stream carries on its journey through the large intestine, where the liquid part of the "soup" is absorbed. The solid waste that remains is passed out of the body through the anus as feces.

① ② ③ ④

So what happens to all that blood laden with little particles of all the terrible things you shouldn't have eaten for lunch? Turn the page and find out!

15

. . . DELIVERING THE GOODS . . . .

Blood is the body's transport system, delivering food, water, and oxygen where they are needed and taking away waste from cells. Blood travels around the body in blood vessels, which range from the larger watertight veins to networks of tiny capillaries. Nutrients and oxygen can trickle through the capillaries into the body's cells, and waste materials can seep back into the blood supply.

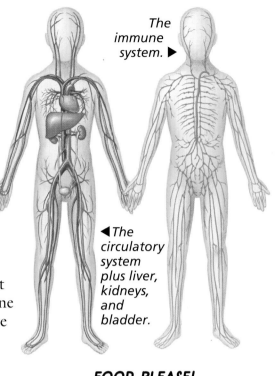

The immune system. ▶

◀ *The circulatory system plus liver, kidneys, and bladder.*

OXYGEN PLEASE!

Every cell in the body needs oxygen: it is the gas that cells need to burn food and turn it into energy. So one of the jobs blood has to do is collect oxygen from the tiny capillaries in the lungs. Oxygenated blood (shown in red in the circulation system diagram) goes to the heart to be pumped around the body.

As blood travels around delivering oxygen, it picks up the exhaust gas (carbon dioxide) and other waste chemicals that cells give off from burning up all that food.

When the blood has given up all its oxygen and is full of carbon dioxide (shown in blue), it makes its way back to the heart, and is pumped directly to the lungs. Here it gives off its exhaust gases that are then breathed out. Blood picks up more oxygen and rushes back to the heart, ready for another circuit.

FOOD PLEASE!

The other life-giving substance our body cells need is food. We saw on pages 14 and 15 how our food gets turned into the kind of material that cells can use. This food enters the bloodstream from the digestive system. On its way from the digestive system back to the heart, blood takes the food and passes it on to the liver for sorting. Another job that the blood does is to dump the chemical and fluid waste picked up on its journey into the kidneys.

KEY
red trucks = blood
yellow dots = oxygen
green dots = nutrients
black bins = waste

Blood delivers oxygen and nutrients to all the cells that make up the various tissues of the body, and collects waste as it passes by.

. . . AND TAKING AWAY WASTE . . .

THE LIVER

The liver has an incredibly complicated job to do. It is a sorting office for the little particles of food, delivering the useful ones back into the blood supply and dealing with poisons and waste matter. It either turns poisons into harmless substances or gets rid of them.

THE KIDNEYS

You have two of these. These bean-shaped organs take the chemical waste and unnecessary water and turn them into urine, which drips into the bladder. When the bladder is full, you feel the need to go to the bathroom and get rid of the waste products from all those energetic food-burning cells.

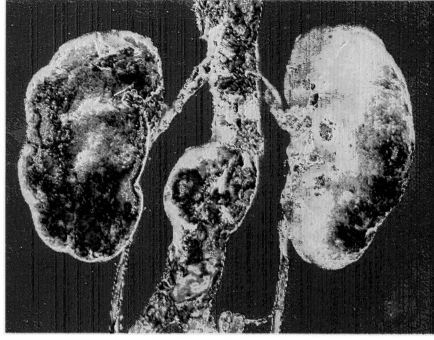

This computer digitized illustration shows a pair of healthy kidneys. They act as a filter for the blood, getting rid of any waste.

YOUR IMMUNE SYSTEM

This is a joint production involving your bone marrow, blood cells, and glands. Glands are like little factories, busy making the chemicals your body needs to fight off disease. Healthy people have immune systems that work well. If the immune system is destroyed or weakened, there's no way a person can stay healthy.

Did I hear someone say, "Where are blood cells 'born'?" You weren't paying attention were you? Go back and look up WHAT'S IN A BONE? on page 8!

Your Busy Blood

✓ In a square inch (6.5 sq cm) patch of muscle tissue, there are more than 1,000,000 capillaries.

✓ Each second, about 8 million blood cells die and the same number are born.

✓ It takes about 20 seconds for a blood cell to circle the whole body.

17

THE HEART

T he heart is a magnificent muscle positioned inside the ribcage between the lungs. The heart is the pump that keeps the blood going around and around the body. It does not sound very romantic, and in fact the heart isn't even "heart-shaped"! It's a complicated bundle of veins and arteries leading into a bag of muscle about the size of an adult fist.

INSIDE THE BAG

The heart is made up of two pumps, separated by an internal wall. The pump on your left-hand side pumps bright red oxygenated blood into the main artery. The blood then goes on its journey around the body.

By the time the blood has been all around the body passing out oxygen, it creeps back along the main vein into the right side of the heart. The right-side pump then sends the dark, purple-colored, exhausted blood on a quick trip to the lungs. Then it comes gushing back into the left side, all bright red and ready for work.

VEINS AND ARTERIES

The blood vessels that carry red oxygenated blood away from the heart to all parts of the body are called arteries. The blood vessels that carry the purplish, exhausted blood back to the heart are called veins.

The heart sends out about two and a half volts of electricity, which is about one-third of the power of a small light bulb.

VALVES

Blood can only go one way. It cannot go backward because the exit points from the heart to the main arteries are guarded by one-way valves that shut tight while the heart is refilling.

FEELING YOUR PULSE

You can feel your blood pumping around your body if you hold your fingers over an artery that is close to the surface of the skin. The places to try are on your wrist and either side of your neck. Normal pulse rate is around 70 beats per minute for an adult and slightly higher for children.

Your Hardworking Heart

✓ The heart beats around 3 billion times in the course of an average life.

✓ The sounds of the heartbeat are made by valves banging shut.

✓ The heart muscle, like all the other muscles in the body, needs exercise to keep healthy. You can exercise your heart by running around a bit everyday so your heart beats faster for a while.

Do you remember what's so special about the heart muscle? Go back to page 13 and have a look. I'm just off to do some exercises.

O xygen, that gas that all our body cells need, is in the air that we breathe. All you have to do to get oxygen into your body is breathe air into your lungs through your nose and mouth. From then on, your body's amazing systems take over. In fact, you don't even have to remember to breathe in and out because your brain takes care of that for you.

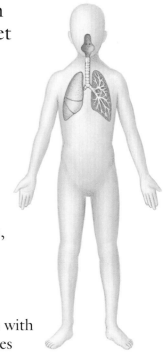

The respiratory system.

FILTERING AND WARMING

Inside your nose, there are lots of little tiny hairs that help to filter out dust and warm the air up a bit; so if it is cold and dusty outside, remember to breathe in through your nose, not your mouth!

BREATHING IN . . .

The air goes down the windpipe (called the trachea), which then branches in two, carrying air into the lungs. Lungs are like sponges with millions of tiny capillaries wrapped around little air sacs. As air rushes into the lungs, the air sacs expand and fill up, and the capillaries can take the oxygen and pass it into the blood stream.

. . . AND BREATHING OUT

As well as grabbing oxygen, the little capillaries are getting rid of waste gas in the form of carbon dioxide. They push this gas into the air sacs and we breathe it out. The exchange of gases is very quick and efficient.

The exhausted blood enters the lungs. Here, it delivers waste collected on its journey, and is given a fresh supply of oxygen.

KEY
red trucks = blood
yellow dots = oxygen
green dots = nutrients
black bins = waste

THE MUSCLES OF BREATHING

The function of lungs is controlled by the diaphragm, a sheet of muscle under the lungs. The brain tells this muscle to go up and down, and when it goes up, it pushes air out of the lungs, and when it goes down, air rushes in.

VOICE BOX

You can speak and sing and shout and whisper all thanks to your voice box, or larynx, which is in your throat, just at the entrance to your windpipe. Sounds are produced when air is pushed over the surface of your vocal cords, which vibrate like guitar strings. Vocal cords are controlled by muscles that tighten and relax, making higher or lower sounds. The sounds are shaped in the mouth by the tongue, teeth, lips, and palate. Say Aaaaah!

A resin cast showing how the windpipe splits into two as it enters the lungs, then divides and subdivides. This allows air to be carried to the millions of tiny air sacs inside the lungs.

Your Lovely Lungs

✓ Healthy lungs can take in huge amounts of air when they need to. Deep breathing is good for the lungs, and so is exercise. The more you exercise, the less winded you will feel the next time you have to run for the school bus.

✓ Your right lung is bigger than your left lung, which has to be a little smaller to make room for your heart.

✓ There are over 300 million air sacs in each lung.

✓ While you are reading this book, you are breathing in and out between 12 and 15 times a minute.

✓ The highest recorded sneeze speed is 103 miles (165.76 km) per hour.

✓ We lose half a quart (almost one liter) of water a day through breathing. This is the water vapor we can see when we breathe onto a mirror.

I don't want to spoil the fun, but did you know that smoking ruins your lungs? Your lungs need oxygen, not dirty smoke. Here's a little tip: if you don't get started, then you won't have to go through the agony of giving it up!

..... THE NERVOUS SYSTEM .....

We have all these wonderful systems in our bodies, but what makes them work? The answer to that is another astonishing system: the nervous system. The control box of the system is the brain, and the brain picks up its information and sends out its messages through a network of nerves running all around the body.

WHAT A NERVE!
Nerves are made up of thousands of tiny nerve cells called neurons. Each cell can receive and send messages, sort of like a radio that picks up signals with its antenna and sends out sounds through its speakers.

IT'S ELECTRIC!
Nerves work by sending out little ripples, like electricity, that stimulate a muscle or organ into action.

The nervous system.

FEELING AND MOVING
You have two kinds of nerves: sensory nerves, which send and receive information, and motor nerves, which make things move.

Sensory nerves alert the brain to pain.

TWO SYSTEMS IN ONE
One part of the nervous system deals with actions that we consciously control, like picking up a pen to write something. The other part deals with all the things that go on automatically, like breathing or digesting food.

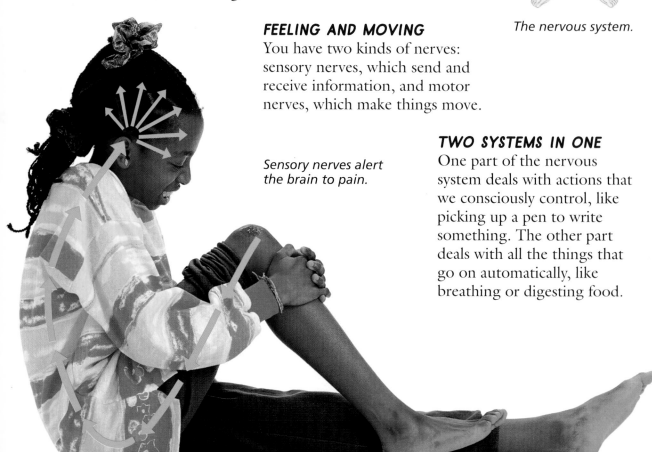

22

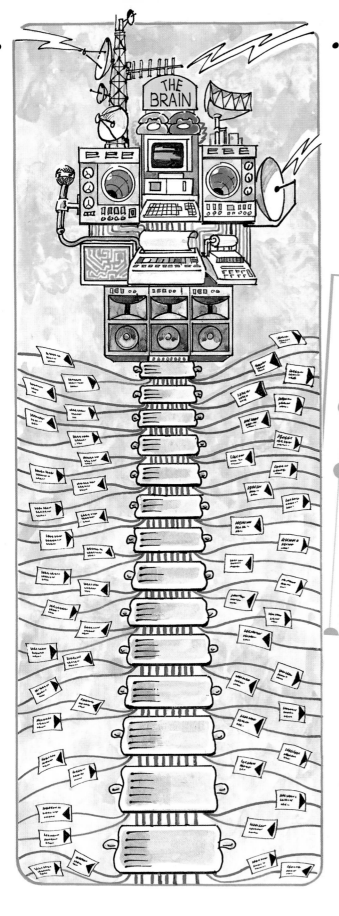

THE NERVE HIGHWAY

The spinal cord is the main bundle of nerves. It acts like a communications highway, with information racing up and down it, and lots of minor roads branching off it. Your spinal cord is a vital part of you and it is protected by your spine. Your spine, or backbone, is made up of individual bones called vertebrae.

Your Networking Nerves

✓ You have 28 billion nerve cells in your body.

✓ The little ripples, called impulses, travel at different speeds. Some idle along at 1.5 mph while others whiz along at 324 mph.

✓ The spinal cord weighs 1.5 oz . It is 17 inches long and almost one inch (2 cm) thick.

✓ Reflex actions are automatic actions that your nervous system handles alone, without asking the brain for permission to act. They include sneezing and blinking.

Some animals on your planet have very well-developed nervous systems, but they don't do much in the way of thinking. Birds aren't called bird-brained for nothing.

. . . . THE SENSES . . . .

Y ou have five senses: hearing, sight, smell, taste and touch. Senses give information from the outside world to your body. Nerves send this information to the brain, and the brain makes sense of it all and decides what to do next. Say, for example, you see and hear a branch falling out of a tree just above you. Your brainy brain will immediately send extra energy to your leg muscles so you can get out of the way quickly!

I HEAR

Obviously this is a job for the ears. Sounds go into your ears and make your eardrums and a collection of little ear bones shake. These shakes, or vibrations, are picked up by nerves and sent back to the brain, which figures out that your alarm has gone off and it's time to get up.

Your Stupendous Senses

✓ Some parts of your body are more sensitive than others. If you touch your body with a set of dividers positioned 1/4 inch apart, most parts of your body will only feel one point. Nose, tongue, and fingertips are the most sensitive parts of the body and in those places you will feel the two points.

I SEE

Eyes are like cameras. Light bounces off the things you see and makes up a pattern. The light goes into your eyes through the dark opening — the pupil. Then it is focused on the back of the eye, where special cells turn this pattern of light into nerve signals. The brain receives this coded message and figures out what you're looking at.

I SMELL

Smells are made up of tiny, invisible particles that hang in the air. We have special little cells inside our noses that can detect the different smells of these particles. The information is fed back to the brain and – you've guessed it – the brain tells you that the bacon cooking in the frying pan is going to taste delicious!

I TASTE

The special cells that detect the taste of things are called taste buds and they are found on your tongue. Humans can tell the difference among only four tastes: sweet, sour, bitter, and salty. Sweet and salty taste buds are on the tip of your tongue, sour on the sides, and bitter at the back. Taste and smell are very closely linked.

I TOUCH

Just under your skin there are millions of tiny nerve endings collecting touch sensations and sending them back to the brain. The brain figures out if you're touching a bowl of ice cubes or stroking the cat.

Human ears are okay, I suppose, but did you know that a fox can hear a worm wriggling on the other side of a field?

CENTRAL CONTROL: THE BRAIN

Your brain looks like a huge, very wrinkled walnut. It sits inside a "box" of bone — your skull — protected from knocks and jolts by a cushion of fluid. It is in charge of everything that happens in the body. It also stores all your memories, and it's where your thoughts and feelings come from. Your brain is YOU.

INSIDE THE BRAIN

The brain is basically a mass of remarkably clever brain cells. Although it looks the same all over, it isn't! Each area of the brain specializes in something different.

LEFT AND RIGHT

The main part of the brain is divided into two halves that work closely together. The left side of the brain takes on most of the work involved in speech, reading and writing, and it controls the muscles on the right side of the body. The right side controls the muscles on the left side, and specializes in working things out and in the relationships between objects or sounds, and space or silence. Musicians and mathematicians usually have well-developed right sides of their brains.

THINKING, FEELING AND MOVING

Between them, the two halves of your brain sort out messages arriving from the sense organs, store information and memories, and allow you to feel and to think, and to control your movement and speech.

FRAGILE

Your brain is like a fragile gift that needs to be carefully wrapped inside a strong box.

If you want to be a healthy person, you have

AUTOMATIC PILOT

The part of the brain nearest to the spinal cord controls the things the body does automatically, like breathing, coughing, sneezing, and digesting food.

DREAM TIME

Some experts think that dreams are the brain's way of sorting out the new things we've learned or experienced during the day before they get filed away in the memory. Most people have about four half-hour dreams a night, but few people remember them all. Some people think you can dream the future, but that is probably just wishful thinking!

Try this trick for remembering telephone numbers by turning them into pictures. Think of numbers 0-9 as these rhyming images: hero, bun, shoe, tree, door, hive, sticks, heaven, gate, line. Then, to remember numbers, just picture them. It's as easy as bun, shoe, tree!

Your Brilliant Brain

✓ The brain feels no pain. It has no cells to sense pain although it is the first to respond when any other part of the body hurts.

✓ The average brain contains 10,000 million brain cells.

✓ Messages travel within the brain at over 250 mph (400 kph).

✓ The brain weighs a little more than 1/2 a pound (0.3 kg).

. . . . HOW CAN I HELP ME? . . . .

Your body needs you! You are its only owner and you're in charge! You can help your heart and muscles to be fit and strong by exercising regularly. You can help your blood and your brain by eating well and avoiding drugs, because drugs go right into the blood stream and confuse your brain. And how is a confused brain going to cope with all the work it has to do work?

BODY MAINTENANCE

Exercise is easy! Just make sure you participate in sports and run around the playground, or swim, or even walk to school every day. It is very important to exercise regularly to make your heart strong and healthy. After you have exercised, find some time to relax. Rest is also vital for a healthy body.

KEEPING CLEAN

Wash regularly to get rid of grease and grime. Otherwise your skin will get infected and you'll get blemishes and uncomfortable rashes. And brush those teeth! If your baby teeth rot, your second teeth won't be healthy, and if your second teeth fall out, that's it! Toothless!

EATING WELL

As you have learned from looking at the digestive system, you are what you eat. So would you rather be made of greasy chips and squashy eclairs, or crispy apples and scrumptious spaghetti? Actually what you need is a balance of different foods and plenty of fresh fruit and vegetables to give your body the kind of fuel it needs.

HAVING FUN

Some people seem to think you can have fun only if you are drunk out of your mind or hanging out with a crowd who smokes. But just think of the dreadful things these people are doing to their bodies. Smoking makes people smelly and sometimes very ill, so where's the fun in that? Drinking too much causes damage to the liver, the brain, and the heart, and other drugs kill brain cells by the million. Where's the sense in that? You need all the brain cells you can get.

On Pluto we don't choose to smoke or take drugs. That's because we're a great deal smarter than some humans! It's worth remembering – you can have a lot more fun if you're healthy and well!

LETTER FROM LIFE EDUCATION

Dear Friends:

The first Life Education Center was opened in Sydney, Australia, in 1979. Founded by the Rev. Ted Noffs, the Life Education program came about as a result of his many years of work with drug addicts and their families.

Ted Noffs realized that preventive education, beginning with children from the earliest possible age all the way into their teenage years, was the only long-term solution to drug abuse and other related problems, including violence and AIDS.

Life Education pioneered the use of technology in a futuristic "Classroom of the 21st Century," designed to show in an exciting way the beauty of life on planet Earth and how drugs including nicotine and alcohol can destroy the delicate balance of human life itself. In every Life Education classroom, there are electronic displays that show the major body systems including the respiratory, nervous, digestive, and immune systems. There is a talking brain and wondrous star ceiling. And there is Harold the Giraffe who appears in many of the programs and is Life Education's official mascot. Programs start in preschool and go all the way through high school.

There are parents' programs and violence prevention classes. Life Education has also begun to create interactive software for home and school computers as well as having its own home page on the Internet, the global information superhighway (the address is http://www.lec.org/).

There are Life Education Centers operating in seven countries (Thailand, the United States, the United Kingdom, New Zealand, Australia, Hong Kong, and New Guinea).

This series of books will allow the wonder and magic of Life Education to reach many more young people with the simple message that each human being is special and unique and that in all of the past, present, and future history there will never be another person exactly the same as you.

If you would like to learn more about Life Education International contact us at one of the addresses listed below or, if you have a computer with a modem, you can write to Harold the Giraffe at Harold@lec.org and you'll find out that a giraffe can send E-mail!

Let's learn to live.

All of us at the Life Education Center.

Life Education, USA
149 Addison Ave
Elmhurst, Illinois
60126
Tel: 708-530-8999
Fax: 708-530-7241

Life Education, UK
20 Long Lane
London
EC1A 9HL
United Kingdom
Tel: 0171-600-6969
Fax: 0171-600-6979

Life Education,
Australia
29 Hughes Street
Potts Point
NSW 2011
Australia
Tel: 0061-2-358-2466
Fax: 0061-2-357-2569

Life Education,
New Zealand
126 The Terrace
PO Box 10-769
Wellington
New Zealand
Tel: 0064-4-472-9620
Fax: 0064-4-472-9609

GLOSSARY

Air sacs Tiny compartments inside your lungs that fill with air when you breathe in.

Arteries Blood vessels that carry oxygenated blood away from the heart and around the body.

Capillaries Fine, hairlike blood vessels. They connect the veins with the arteries.

Cartilage The special covering that protects the ends of your bones.

Glands Organs in the body that make substances needed by your body.

Joint Where two or more bones meet. You have two types of joints: hinge joints and ball and socket joints.

Ligaments These attach bones to other bones.

Neurons Nerve cells – your nerves are made up of many thousands of these.

Puberty When your reproductive organs start to develop. If you are a girl, you begin to become a woman. If you are a boy, you begin to become a man.

Pulse The feel of your blood throbbing as it is pumped around your body along the arteries.

Saliva A liquid produced by your salivary glands. It softens up your food, making it easier to swallow.

Taste buds Tiny bumps on your tongue that allow you to taste salty, sweet, sour, and bitter flavors.

Tendons These attach bones to muscles.

Veins Blood vessels that carry the used blood back to the heart.

Windpipe The main passage that takes air from your nose or mouth down into the lungs.

FURTHER INFORMATION

These organizations can help you with your questions:

American Heart Association
7272 Greenville Avenue
Dallas, TX 75321
Telephone: 214-373-6300
Toll-free: 800-242-8721
Fax: 214-706-1341

American Lung Association
1740 Broadway
New York, NY 10019
Telephone: 212-315-8700
Fax: 212-265-5642

President's Council on Physical Fitness and Sports
701 Pennsylvania Avenue, NW
Suite 250
Washington, DC 20004
Telephone: 202-272-3421
Fax: 202-504-2064

TARGET
Helping Students Cope with Tobacco, Alcohol, and Other Drugs
11724 NW Plaza Circle
PO Box 20626
Kansas City, MO 64195
Telephone: 816-464-5400
Toll-free: 800-366-6667
Fax: 816-464-5571